CHRISTMAS

A-Z: EVERYTHING ABOUT CHRISTMAS

Happy Holidays!

 **IS FOR**

Angel

B b IS FOR

Santa Tours

BUS

C C IS FOR

Crystal Ball

 **IS FOR**

Down the chimney

Ee IS FOR

Elf

Ff IS FOR

Fireplace

Gg IS FOR

Gingerbread man

Hh IS FOR

Hot cocoa

Ii

IS FOR

Ice skating

Jj IS FOR

Jingle Bell

 IS FOR

knitted sweater

Ll IS FOR

Lights

Mm IS FOR

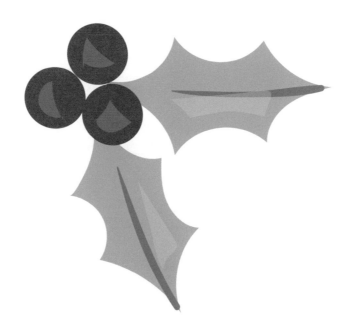

Mistletoe

Nn IS FOR

Nutcracker

Oo IS FOR

Owl

Pp IS FOR

Present

Qq IS FOR

Quilt

Rr IS FOR

Reindeer

 IS FOR

Sleigh

T t IS FOR

Train

Uu IS FOR

Unicorn

V V IS FOR

Village

W w IS FOR

Wreath

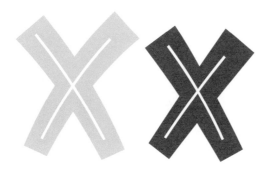 IS FOR

X-mas tree

Yy IS FOR

Yummy treats

Zz IS FOR

Zzz

Made in United States
Troutdale, OR
12/09/2023